MICHAEL TIPPETT

FANTASIA CONCERTANTE

on a theme of Corelli
for String Orchestra

D0503890

Ernst Eulenburg Ltd

London · Mainz · Madrid · New York · Paris · Tokyo · Toronto · Zürich

PREFACE/VORWORT

Tippett's *Fantasia Concertante on a theme of Corelli* was commissioned by the Edinburgh Festival Society in celebration of the tercentenary of the birth of Corelli (1653–1713) and first performed on 29 August 1953 in the Usher Hall during that year's Edinburgh Festival. The BBC Symphony Orchestra was conducted by the composer, the solo violin parts being played by Maria Lidka and John Glickman, the solo cello by Peter Muscant, at that time principal cellist of the orchestra.

At the 1953 Edinburgh Festival a special feature was made of music for the violin and violin family (and hence of the music of Italy), and several concerts were given under the heading of 'Four Centuries of the Violin'. As Robert Ponsonby wrote in the festival handbook, the first composer who had fully grasped the potentialities of the instrument was Corelli. It was appropriate therefore that his tercentenary should have been celebrated with a work newly written for the occasion.

When he received the commission (for a fee of £100), in July 1952, Tippett was still composing his first opera, *The Midsummer Marriage*. He accepted it because he liked writing for strings, and was thinking of writing something for strings anyway after his exertions on the opera. He was also attracted to the idea of reviving the brilliant, baroque style of violin writing he had always admired in such composers as Corelli, Purcell, Bach and Handel. An added attraction, at a stage in his career when performances of his music were infrequent, was a guaranteed second performance at the 1953 Promenade Concerts. (This duly took place, on 3 September in the Royal Albert Hall,

Tippetts *Fantasia Concertante on a theme of Corelli* war ein Auftragswerk der Edinburgh Festival Society anläßlich des 300. Geburtstages von Corelli (1653–1713) und wurde am 29. August 1953 während des Edinburgh Festivals uraufgeführt. Das BBC Symphony Orchestra leitete der Komponist selbst, die Geigen-Soli spielten Maria Lidka und John Glickman, das Cello-Solo Peter Muscant, der damalige Solocellist des Orchesters.

Das Edinburgh Festival 1953 war insbesondere der Musik für Geige und der Geigenfamilie (somit auch der italienischen Musik) gewidmet, und mehrere Konzerte fanden unter dem Titel *Vier Jahrhunderte der Geige* statt. Wie in dem Begleitheft zum Festival von Robert Ponsonby angemerkt wurde, war Corelli der erste Komponist, der die Möglichkeiten der Geige völlig erfaßte. Deswegen war es auch angemessen, seinen 300. Geburtstag mit einem Auftragswerk zu begehen.

Tippett war noch dabei, seine erste Oper *The Midsummer Marriage* zu schreiben, als er im Juli 1952 den Auftrag für dieses Werk erhielt (sein Honorar betrug 100 Englische Pfund) und den er annahm, weil er gerne für Streichinstrumente schrieb und weil er ohnehin vorgehabt hatte, nach den Anstrengungen der Oper ein Stück für Streicher zu schreiben. Auch die Wiederbelebung des brillianten barocken Geigenstils, den er schon immer bei Komponisten wie Corelli, Purcell, Bach und Händel bewundert hatte, war für ihn reizvoll. Er befand sich in einem Stadium seiner Karriere, wo Aufführungen seiner Werke relativ selten waren, und die zugesicherte

IV

with the same performers as at the first performance.)

In order to find a feasible starting point for his new work, Tippett had examined Corelli's twelve Concerti Grossi Op. 6 and eventually selected an excerpt from the first movement of No. 2 in F: an *adagio* of a 'dark, passionate kind', as he described it in a programme note, and a *vivace*, in which Corelli 'explores the brilliance of the violin'.[1] This 'theme' is illustrated below. (Corelli's principal material, indicated within square brackets, Tippett ignored.) A friend informed him that Bach had written an organ fugue on a theme by Corelli (BWV 579),[2] and he was pleased at the prospect of stiffening the Corelli with some Bach, not least because this also enabled him to develop a compositional idea he had found in Beethoven's Diabelli Variations for piano – of writing a variations and fugue in which the fugue is not placed last. In turn this enabled him to put another compositional idea in practice – of writing a modern equivalent of the gentle *siciliano* style in the Pastorale at the end of Corelli's 'Christmas Concerto', Op. 6 No. 8, or in a similar piece he was very fond of, the Pastoral Symphony in Handel's *Messiah*. These were the plans Tippett had assembled before he started composition. He realized them all, even if the design of the eventual *Fantasia Concertante* bears a closer resemblance to the designs of the viol fantasias of Purcell than to a conventional

zweite Aufführung im Rahmen der Promenaden Konzerte 1953 bedeutete für ihn einen zusätzlichen Anreiz. (Dieses Konzert fand auch am 3. September 1953 in der Royal Albert Hall statt, unter Mitwirkung derselben Musiker wie bei der Uraufführung.)

Um sich eine Ausgangsbasis für sein neues Werk zu verschaffen, hatte Tippett die zwölf Concerti Grossi op. 6 von Corelli studiert und sich zwei Ausschnitte daraus ausgesucht: aus dem ersten Satz von Nr. 2 in F ein ,,dunkles, leidenschaftliches" *Adagio*, wie er es im Programmheft beschrieb, und ein *Vivace*, in dem Corelli ,,die Brillianz der Geige erforscht"[1]. Dieses Thema ist unten wiedergegeben. (Corellis Hauptthema – hier in eckigen Klammern – wurde von Tippett nicht berücksichtigt.) Ein Freund teilte ihm mit, daß Bach eine Fuge für Orgel auf ein Thema von Corelli (BWV 579)[2] geschrieben hätte, und Tippett freute sich über die Möglichkeit, das thematische Material von Corelli mit Bachschem Material zu verstärken, nicht zuletzt weil dieses Material es ihm ermöglichte, eine andere kompositorische Idee, die er in den Diabelli-Variationen von Beethoven gefunden hatte, zu verwirklichen – nämlich Variationen und Fuge, in denen die Fuge nicht als Finale plaziert war. Dadurch ergab sich wiederum die Mo glichkeit, eine weitere Idee auszuführen: ein modernes Gegenstück zum sanften *Siciliano* der Pastorale am Schluß von Corellis ,,Weihnachtskonzert" op. 6, Nr. 8, und zu einem seiner Lieblingsstücke – der Pastoral-Sinfonia aus dem *Messias* von Händel – zu schreiben. Diese Pläne hatte Tippett gesammelt, bevor er an die komposito-

---

[1] First printed in *Festival Notes*, March 1953, a news bulletin of the Edinburgh Festival

[2] This is an elaborate reworking of the theme from the second movement, a *vivace*, from Corelli's Trio Sonata in B minor, Op. 3 No. 4

[1] Erstmals veröffentlicht in *Festival Notes*, März 1953, einem Nachrichtenblatt des Edinburgh Festivals

[2] Dieses ist eine sorgfältige, reich verzierte Ausarbeitung des Themas aus Corellis Trio-Sonata in h-Moll, op. 3 Nr. 4, zweiter Satz, *Vivace*.

theme and variations. Composition began in early January 1953 and took no more than six weeks, being complete by late February.

rische Arbeit ging. Er hat sie alle realisieren können, obwohl der Aufbau der endgültigen Fassung der *Fantasia Concertante* mehr Ähnlichkeit mit den Gamben-Fantasien von Purcell aufweist als mit dem konventionellen „Thema mit Variationen". Die Kompositionsarbeit

VI

Preparations for the first performance did not proceed so smoothly. Tippett sent a copy of his score to Sir Malcolm Sargent (1895–1967) – who, as chief conductor of the BBC Symphony Orchestra, was due to conduct the first performance in one of the orchestra's Edinburgh concerts that year – adding a short letter saying that here, in contrast to previous Tippett works Sargent had conducted, was a 'nice, romantic piece' that should appeal to him. Sargent however was hostile to the work, thinking there were too many notes which did not add up. He was ready to agree with the suggestion that if it was thought too difficult for him, the composer should conduct – which accounts for his remark at an Edinburgh press conference two days before the first performance: 'People like to see the composer conducting but usually it is not good.'

Press reviews of the first performances were mixed, largely because the 'furious contrapuntal complexity'[3] at the climax of the fugue was found either contrived or incomprehensible. Yet several critics acknowledged the quality of the work: 'One could call it intellectual if that did not generally imply that it was not beautiful, and it strikingly is.'[4] '[. . .] an involved sonorous mesh, which all but succeeds in hiding the essentially fine and

hat er Anfang Januar 1953 begonnen; sie erstreckte sich auf nur sechs Wochen und war gegen Ende Februar beendet.

Die Vorbereitungen für die Uraufführung liefen nicht so glatt. Tippett schickte eine Kopie des Stückes an Sir Malcolm Sargent (1895–1967), der in jenem Jahr als leitender Dirigent des BBC Symphony Orchestra für die Uraufführung in dem Edinburger Konzert verpflichtet worden war. Er fügte einen kurzen Brief hinzu, in dem er das Werk in den Gegensatz zu den früheren Werken stellte, die von Sir Malcolm schon dirigiert worden waren, und es als ,,nettes, romantisches Stück" anbot, das ihm bestimmt gefallen würde. Sargent jedoch war von der Komposition nicht angetan; er meinte, es habe zu viele Töne, die nicht ,,aufgingen". Er war mit dem Vorschlag einverstanden, daß – falls das Werk ihm zu schwierig schien – der Komponist dirigieren sollte. Damit erklärt sich auch seine Bemerkung in einer Pressekonferenz zwei Tage vor der Uraufführung: ,,Das Publikum sieht es gerne, wenn der Komponist dirigiert, aber es ist nicht gut."

Die Pressestimmen zur Uraufführung waren gemischt, hauptsächlich wegen ,,der wilden kontrapunktischen Verwicklungen"[3] im Höhepunkt der Fuge, die als künstlich oder unverständlich beurteilt worden waren. Es waren jedoch einige Kritiker, die die Qualitäten des Werkes anerkannten: ,,Man könnte es für ein intellektuelles Stück erklären, wenn dieses nicht auch bedeuten würde, daß es nicht wunderschön sei, und das ist es: auffällig und eindrucksvoll."[4] ,,[. . .] ein ineinander verwobenes Klanggebilde, welches alles andere als die im wesentlichen feine und vorwärtstreibende

[3] Desmond Shawe Taylor, *New Statesman*, 5 September 1953
[4] Colin Mason, *Manchester Guardian*, 31 August 1953

[3] Desmond Shawe Taylor, *New Statesman*, 5. September 1953
[4] Colin Mason, *Manchester Guardian*, 31. August 1953

moving quality of its thought.'[5] '[. . .] showing a concentrated mastery and the profoundest originality. Nobody else writes at all as he does.'[6]

As the first major work Tippett wrote after *The Midsummer Marriage* (1946–52), his *Fantasia Concertante* is strongly influenced by the expressive world of the opera. It contains similar alternations between the 'dark' and the 'light' (here, between the *adagio* and the *vivace* elements in the theme) and a similar concentration on lyrical fervour and luxuriance. Yet it is not a mere appendage to the opera. Its lyricism is richer and warmer than anywhere else in his output and its fantasia design marks a new departure in Tippett's formal thinking, which was to culminate in the fantasia-like construction of his second opera, *King Priam* (1958–61).

The *Fantasia Concertante* is laid out in five main sections. The first comprises the theme and two variations: the second (from fig. 16) is an exploration of the 'dark' and the 'light' (this latter, five divisions on a ground); the third (fig. 39) a variation on the original *adagio*; the fourth (fig. 46) a fugue on the Bach subject with two counter-subjects of Tippett's own; the fifth (one bar before fig. 79) a Pastorale. The work concludes with a miniature coda returning to the Corelli material.

For the first edition of the score, published in 1953, Tippett provided the following note:
'The string orchestra (which can be of

Eigenart des musikalischen Gedankens verhehlen kann."[5] ,,[. . .] zeigt eine ausgeprägte Meisterschaft und eine tiefgründige Originalität. Keiner schreibt so wie er."[6]

Als erstes bedeutendes Werk nach der Oper *The Midsummer Marriage* (1946–52) geschrieben, weist die *Fantasia Concertante* eine starke Beeinflussung von der expressiven Welt der Oper auf. Es beinhaltet einen ähnlichen Wechsel zwischen ,,dunkel" und ,,hell" (hier zwischen *Adagio*- und *Vivace*-Elementen des Themas) und ein ähnliche Konzentration lyrischer Glut und Üppigkeit. Es ist aber nicht als ein Anhängsel der Oper zu sehen. Die Lyrik dieses Stückes ist reichhaltiger und wärmer als in seinen anderen Werken, und die Struktur der *Fantasia* leitet einen neuen Abschnitt in Tippetts formalem Denken ein – einen Abschnitt, der seinen Höhepunkt in der fantasieähnlichen Ausarbeitung seiner zweiten Oper, *King Priam* (1958–61) erlebt.

Die *Fantasie Concertante* ist in fünf Hauptabschnitte angelegt. Der erste Teil beinhaltet das Thema und zwei Variationen; der zweite (ab Ziffer 16) ist eine Erforschung des ,,Dunklen" und des ,,Hellen" (letzteres beträgt fünf Abschnitte auf einem Basso Ostinato); der dritte Teil ist (Ziffer 39) eine Variation des ursprünglichen *Adagio*; der vierte Teil (Ziffer 46) eine Fuge über das Bachsche Thema, mit zwei Kontrasubjekten von Tippett; der fünfte Teil (ein Takt vor Ziffer 79) ein Pastorale. Das Werk endet mit einer kurzen Coda, wiederum aus dem Corelli-Zitat herausgearbeitet.

Zu der ersten Ausgabe des Werkes 1953 schrieb Tippett folgende Anmerkungen:
,,Das Streichorchester (welches von

---

[5] Felix Aprahamian, *The Sunday Times*, 6 September 1953
[6] Eric Blom, *The Observer*, 13 September 1953

[5] Felix Aprahamian, *The Sunday Times*, 6. September 1953
[6] Eric Blom, *The Observer,* 13. September 1953

any size) is divided into three parts. 1° Concertino, two solo violins and solo cello; 2° Concerto Grosso, roughly one half of the remaining string body; 3° Concerto Terzo, the other half.

'The theme is taken from Corelli's Concerto Grosso Op. 6 No. 2, and in the *Fantasia Concertante* appears as the first twenty-one bars of the Concertino and Concerto Grosso.

'While at first the Concerto Terzo plays the part of instruments accompanying from the figured bass, it later assumes a role equal to the Concerto Grosso. The tripartite division is abandoned altogether in the Fugue (fig. 46) which itself incorporates a partial transcription of the first twelve [eleven] bars of Bach's double fugue on themes of Corelli (BWV 579).'

Ian Kemp

beliebiger Größe sein darf), wird in drei Teile aufgeteilt: 1. Concertino – zwei Sologeigen, ein Solocello; 2. Concerto Grosso – etwa die Hälfte der bleibenden Streicher; 3. Concerto Terzo – die andere Hälfte.

Das Thema ist dem Concerto Grosso op. 6 Nr. 2 von Corelli entnommen. In der *Fantasia Concertante* erscheint es in den ersten einundzwanzig Takten von Concertino und Concerto Grosso.

Zunächst spielt das Concerto Terzo die Rolle des Tasteninstrumentes im Basso Continuo, später übernimmt es eine gleichwertige Rolle mit dem Concerto Grosso. Die dreifache Aufteilung wird in der Fuge (Ziffer 46) verlassen. Die Fuge beinhaltet eine partielle Transkription der ersten zwölf [elf] Takte aus Bachs Doppelfuge auf Themen von Corelli (BWV 579)."

Ian Kemp
Übersetzung Norma Enns

Orchestral layout/Anordnung des Orchesters

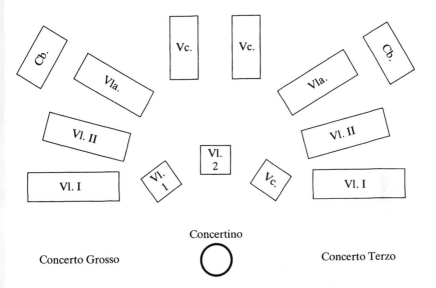

Concertino

Concerto Grosso   Concerto Terzo

FANTASIA CONCERTANTE
on a theme of Corelli

Michael Tippett
(1905–)

No. 1395   EE 6697

2

5

6

EE 6697

8

12

14

16

19 **poco più tranquillo** ♩ = c.66 (Andante)

EE 6697

93
24
Vl. 1
Vl. 2
Vc.
Vl.
Vla.
Vc.
Cb.
Vl.
Vla.
Vc
Cb.
f
mp
cresc.
(mf)
mp cresc.
molto
p
(mp)

32

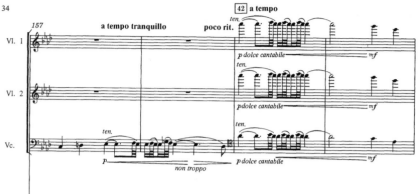

38

FUGUE

46

173   **Allegro moderato (♩ = 96-100)**   47

178

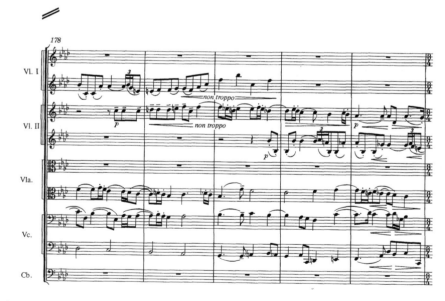

EE 6697

44

48

EE 6697

Andante – Adagio alla pastorale tranquilla ♪ = c.92

54

EE 6697

60

89 **Andante - Allegretto appassionato** ♩ = c.66

62